2nd edition

Introduction Health and Mental Wellbeing for Staff Supporting Adults with Intellectual Disabilities

A guide for professionals, support staff and families

Eddie Chaplin, Karina Marshall-Tate, Steve Hardy & Ruwani Ampegama

London
South Bank
University

*e*stia centre

Pavilion

Introduction to Mental Health and Mental Wellbeing for Staff
Supporting Adults with Intellectual Disabilities: A guide for
professionals, support staff and families

© Pavilion Publishing & Media Ltd

The authors have asserted their rights in accordance with the
Copyright, Designs and Patents Act (1988) to be identified
as the authors of this work.

Published by:
Pavilion Publishing and Media Ltd
Blue Sky Offices Shoreham
Shoreham-by-Sea, West Sussex BN43 5FF
Tel: 01273 434 943
Email: info@pavpub.com
Web: www.pavpub.com

Published 2020

A catalogue record for this book is available from the
British Library.

ISBN: 978-1-912755-83-7

Pavilion is the leading publisher and provider of professional
development products and services for workers in the health,
social care, education and community safety sectors. We
believe that everyone has the right to fulfil their potential and
we strive to supply products and services that help raise
standards, promote best practices and support continuing
professional development.

Authors: Eddie Chaplin, Karina Marshall-Tate, Steve Hardy
& Ruwani Ampegama

Editor: Ruth Chalmers, Pavilion Publishing and Media Ltd

Design: Emma Dawe, Pavilion Publishing and Media Ltd

Cover: Phil Morash, Pavilion Publishing and Media Ltd

Printing: CMP Digital Print Solutions

Contents

Section 3: Mental health assessment for people with intellectual disabilities 28

Section 4: Mental health interventions and treatment for people with intellectual disabilities 35

Section 5: Mental health promotion and the views of people with intellectual disabilities 43

About the authors

Professor Eddie Chaplin is Professor in the Health and Social Care Department at London South Bank University. He has extensive clinical experience managing and working in a range of local and national mental health services for people with intellectual disabilities and autism. Eddie is Editor for the *Advances in Autism* journal, and recently published the first guided self-help manual specifically aimed at people with intellectual disabilities and autism. His research interests include offending by people with neurodevelopmental disorders and mental health promotion and training via co-production. Eddie is the Secretary of the European Association on Mental Health in Intellectual Disability (EAMHID).

Karina Marshall-Tate is a Consultant Nurse in Intellectual disabilities at South London & Maudsley NHS Foundation Trust. She has led and managed specialist inpatient and community health services for people with an intellectual disability with additional mental illness or behaviours that challenge. Karina is interested in developing education and training for health and care staff about meeting the health needs of people with an intellectual disability.

Steve Hardy qualified as an Intellectual Disability Nurse in 1994 and has worked in both clinical and educational settings. He is currently an Independent Consultant Nurse for People with Learning Disabilities. Sharing information and developing resources is his keen passion. He is widely published around the mental health needs of people with an intellectual disability, capacity and facilitating a platform for people with an intellectual disability to be heard.

Ruwani Ampegama joined the Estia centre in May 2019 as the Senior Training Officer and she is now the Head of Education and Training. She qualified as an intellectual disability nurse in 1993 and completed a BA Honours in Health and Social Care practice at University of Kent in 2006. Following this she also completed a Post Graduate Certificate in Education in 2009 at University of Canterbury Christchurch. She has extensive experience working in a variety of roles including management in community, residential and supported-living settings for people with an intellectual disability and complex needs. She is passionate about supporting and empowering people with an intellectual disability and addressing health inequalities.

Introduction

People with intellectual disabilities are more likely to suffer from mental health problems than the rest of the population for a wide variety of reasons. Coupled with this, noticing and diagnosing a mental illness may be complex, and getting the right kind of help and support can be challenging. This guide has been written for a range of support workers and professionals who may come into contact with people with intellectual disabilities. It aims to raise their awareness of mental health problems, the relationship between intellectual disability and mental health, and the vital support that they might be able to provide, both in promoting good mental health and in helping individuals with intellectual disabilities who have mental health issues.

This guide uses common language in order to demystify mental health and illness in the lives of people with intellectual disability. The content is varied and contains a number of case studies to illustrate the different areas of this resource. The terms 'mental health problems' or 'mental illness' are often used interchangeably outside of clinical environments, and also when talking about people with intellectual disabilities. For the purpose of this booklet we will use the term 'mental health problems' to talk about mental ill health, and the terms 'mental illness' and 'mental disorder' for those whose symptoms are sufficient to get a diagnosis. The following categories of mental disorder are covered – challenging behaviour, mood disorders like depression and anxiety, psychotic disorders like schizophrenia, personality disorder, and dementia, along with advice on how to support the person in their day to day life.

The booklet is divided into four main sections.

In **Section 1**, we explore what we mean by mental health and how it can affect the whole person, including their physical health. This section also addresses common myths surrounding mental health, the relationship between intellectual disability and mental health, and the additional problems that people with intellectual disabilities may have that can prevent or impede them from getting the help and support they need.

Section 2 looks at common mental illnesses and mental disorders, and explores further how people with intellectual disabilities' experience of mental illness can be atypical and more difficult to identify as a result.

Section 3 looks at assessment of mental health from a multi-professional approach and how to support people with intellectual disability to access assessment, care and treatments.

Section 4 looks specifically at common mental health interventions and treatments in common use for people with intellectual disabilities, with emphasis on best and least restrictive practice.

Section 5 covers the strategies that promote resilience and positive mental health in people with intellectual disabilities. It explores what people with intellectual disabilities say about things that help them to look after and improve their mental wellbeing. It offers advice to professionals and others on how best to treat and support someone with a mental health problem.

Throughout these sections the booklet contains a series of case studies that follow people's experience of mental health from identification through to getting treatment.

A note about terminology

While 'learning disability' may be the preferred and familiar term within the UK, it does not have the same meaning in other countries. For clarity, we have used the term 'intellectual disability' rather than 'learning disability' throughout this guide as the former is the most commonly used and understood term around the world.

Section 1:

What is mental health?

Introduction

Good mental health is something most of us take for granted. When we are threatened by our emotions and vulnerable to poor mental health, we often leave ourselves at further risk by minimising and failing to acknowledge our feelings. We often do this out of a fear that others will think that we are being weak and that poor mental health is something that happens to others. As a result, people with mental health issues are often poorly equipped to deal with their situation as they lack strategies to cope with their emotions and feelings.

Section 1 explains what mental health is and how it can affect individuals' everyday life. We will talk about common myths about mental illness, the relationship between mental illness and intellectual disability, and what people can start to do to look after their mental health.

What is mental health?

Mental health is defined as a state of wellbeing in which every individual realises his or her own potential, can cope with the normal stresses of life, can work productively and fruitfully, and is able to make a contribution to her or his community (WHO, 2014).

Mental health problems affect everyone from all walks of life, regardless of their status and circumstances. As many as a quarter of people will experience mental health problems at some time in their life.

The severity of mental health problems and illness varies between people and over time. So a person with a severe mental illness such as schizophrenia can also experience good mental health when not unwell. Mental health problems may be a reaction to life events such as loss, relationship or work problems, or there may be no cause that the person is aware of.

Mental health affects people of all ages and impacts on how people feel, their thoughts and their actions. How we choose to react to our thoughts and feelings can be both positive and negative, and it can affect our emotional, psychological and social wellbeing. Having good mental health allows us to enjoy and appreciate the things around us as well as other people, and allows us to make the most of our relationships. It also helps our self-esteem and sense of belonging, as well as making us more confident in our everyday lives and able to maintain a normal routine, including things most people take for granted such as personal care, shopping and paying bills.

Support will often come from a variety of sources including friends, family, carers and, in some cases, charities. The level of support required is often linked to the person's level of independence and how they are able to manage. Some people with intellectual disabilities will therefore live with family, others independently, and others in supported accommodation which can be anything from a service tailored towards an individual to services with a high level of support and shared living.

Whether someone has a diagnosis of mental illness or not can be irrelevant, as many people with mental health issues or problems find that their condition can be as debilitating in terms of the effect on their day-to-day life whether or not it is formally diagnosed.

There are many things that can trigger mental health problems, from facing everyday stresses such as coping without support, bullying and having our choices limited. There are also other things that affect our mental health including:

- Our life experiences (neglect and abuse).
- Mental health problems within the family.
- Physical factors including our genes and some physical illnesses.

Whatever the cause, when our mental wellbeing is threatened it will change the way we look at things and the decisions we make, for example stopping doing the things we enjoy, coping with stress and taking care of ourselves. This can mean we eat more or less or the wrong things, or people may use alcohol or drugs to cope. Because the person's behaviour changes at these times there is also the problem of how we socialise and there can be difficulties looking after our relationships.

There are a number of factors that are thought to increase a person's vulnerability to mental illness:

- Chronic or acute stress.
- Physical make up such as genetics, body and brain chemistry and hormones.
- Use of alcohol and drugs, both legal and illegal.
- Thinking patterns – how we deal with problems and negative thoughts and what we think about ourselves.
- Social factors such as being out of work, being isolated from others, life events such as break ups or the end of relationships e.g. a support worker leaving.

Common symptoms of mental illness include:

- Feeling lethargic, lacking energy and motivation.
- Negative thoughts and feelings of helplessness.
- Problems concentrating.
- Eating too much or too little.
- Sleeping too much or too little.
- Emotional or tense and experiencing mood swings.
- Constantly worried, nervous or scared, which may cause conflict in everyday situations.
- Physical symptoms such as racing pulse, feeling sick, feeling that there is something physically wrong.
- Unpleasant thoughts that a person can't stop thinking about and cause them stress (ruminations).
- Hearing voices that are not there (hallucinations).
- Having false beliefs about everyday situations that are not true (delusions).
- Thinking of harming or hurting yourself.
- Irrational fear and panic.

These changes in how a person behaves and acts can act as early warning signs.

With the right support in their everyday life, people can overcome many of these problems, including those with intellectual disabilities. For some this will mean changing their lifestyle and routine, much in the way someone trying to get fit would increase their exercise. Indeed, in the UK the NHS promotes mental wellbeing among the population with the 'Five Steps to Wellbeing'. These five steps are:

- **Connect** – with people around you.
- **Be active** – take a walk, find an activity that you enjoy doing.
- **Keep learning** – learning new skills can give you a sense of achievement and a new confidence.
- **Give to others** – even the smallest act can count, whether it's a smile, a thank you or a kind word.
- **Be mindful** – be more aware of the present moment, including your feelings and thoughts, your body and the world around you (NHS Choices, 2014).

By incorporating these steps into everyday life mental wellbeing can be improved.

For some, however, outside help may be needed to help understand how to incorporate this in daily living. This may also include getting treatment and learning strategies to improve their mental wellbeing. Without help it may be difficult for the person to cope with everyday situations and realise their full potential. No one is entirely sure of what causes mental health problems, and unlike physical health problems there is not often a test that confirms a diagnosis. However, to combat this questionnaires have been developed that record the presence of symptoms and their severity, which will assist in the diagnostic process.

Common myths

Not so long ago that it was widely accepted that people with intellectual disabilities did not suffer from or experience mental health problems. This myth originates from the idea that people with intellectual disability were incapable of feelings. Their actions and behaviours were thought to be entirely down to their intellectual disability. Today it is widely accepted that people with intellectual disability are in fact *more* vulnerable to a range of mental illnesses and problems than the rest of the population. A lack of opportunities compared to others often increases their vulnerability. It is estimated that as many as one in four people will suffer with mental health problems, while it is generally accepted that, for people with intellectual disability, this figure is higher.

For many, getting help is often the hardest thing, whether it is due to a lack of support accessing services or gaining support that is appropriate. Despite a growing awareness, people with mental health problems still feel stigmatised by society, making it more difficult to come forward for help.

Common myths and perceptions around mental health problems can often make this worse and discourage people from seeking help.

Myth 1: Mental health problems are the person's own fault

There is an important difference between taking responsibility and accepting blame, but unfortunately many people confuse these two things. Often it is wrongly insinuated that people are in some way to blame for their mental health problems. While we would agree that individuals do need to take responsibility for their thoughts and feelings, they are not to blame for them.

Myth 2: Mental health problems are for life

People can often assume that mental health problems are for life because of a lack of available information. How long will I need to keep having treatment? What can I expect when I am feeling better? Will side effects of medication make me feel worse? Some mental illnesses can occur once in a lifetime, others may come and go.

Myth 3: I don't need any help with my mental health

When they feel they are becoming unwell, many people may rely on coping strategies they have developed. For many people with intellectual disabilities, however, it is hard to recognise their feelings and emotions and to know whether something is wrong and what affect it is having on their day-to-day life. It is also difficult for them to implement coping strategies without additional support. Seeking help is a healthy response and not a sign of weakness. It is often good to get advice from family, carers or support staff about what to do and to get reassurance. People sometimes think that if they admit to having problems they will be considered 'mad', but this is not the case.

Myth 4: Physical problems and ill health are nothing to do with mental health

People with intellectual disability make up around 1.5 to 2% of the world's population and are at increased risk of both mental and physical illness. We know that physical health is linked to our mental wellbeing, and this is reflected in WHO's definition: 'Health is a state of complete physical, mental and social wellbeing and not merely the absence of disease or infirmity'. Knowing that mental health can affect our physical health and physical health can affect our mental health can help us understand more about ourselves. For example, think about when you have felt stressed or angry, you may have also experienced muscle pains in the neck and shoulders and headaches. Likewise, people with long term conditions such as diabetes may be more susceptible to feelings of depression or anxiety because of changes to their lifestyle and worries about how an activity might affect the condition.

It is also the case that those on certain medications for mental health problems may be at increased risk due to possible side effects. For example, the use of antipsychotics can increase the risk of obesity, diabetes and a number of other conditions.

Can having intellectual disabilities affect a person's mental health?

Intellectual disability is not a mental illness, but is a lifelong condition that affects learning and the retention of new information. For many people with intellectual disabilities, it is often a hidden condition that may not be obvious to those around them. The reality is that many people with intellectual disabilities are able to live independently and never come to the attention of services.

Research carried out into the mental health needs of people with intellectual disabilities has shown that they are more likely to experience mental ill-health than the wider population. The causes of this are multiple and include biological, social and psychological vulnerabilities. When treating a person with intellectual disability for a mental health problem, adaptations to treatment may have to be made.

Intellectual disability is often classified by services according to a person's abilities, and is labelled mild, moderate or severe. Additionally, the impact of having intellectual disabilities can make it more difficult for someone to help themselves, for example by doing the NHS's 'Five Steps to Wellbeing', because of the effects on learning and retaining information. This means that the role of the support worker is vital to achieving maximum wellbeing.

How does having an intellectual disability affect a person day-to-day?

The effects of intellectual disabilities will differ from person to person. This is why holistic, person-centred care is so important. However, there are key areas where difficulties can be seen, although the presentation and level of support required will vary.

Communication

Communication is a vital component of all human interactions and intellectual disabilities affect the way that an individual expresses him/herself (expressive communication) and how they understand others (receptive communication). This will affect how the person undertakes daily activities and how they interact socially and relate to others around them. Common communication difficulties can include:

- Memory recall.
- Telling the time.

- Following instructions.
- Concentration.
- Understanding what is expected of them in social situations.

Communication difficulties are not always obvious and the person may try to mask this for fear of failure or looking 'silly'. They may do this by repeating learnt phrases in a rote fashion, or being suggestible and/or acquiescent, agreeing to something usually with the intention to please because they think that is what is required.

For some people, simple alterations in communication can accommodate any difficulties, while for others complex systems of augmented communication may be required after assessment by a speech and language therapist (SLT). Common adaptations to enhance communication include:

- using plain English – no jargon, abbreviations or metaphors
- keeping sentences short, ideally with one idea per sentence
- using simple vocabulary and concepts
- using positive language wherever possible – for example, say, 'We can go swimming after lunch' rather than ' you can't go swimming until we've had lunch'
- using photos, pictures or symbols to enhance communication
- allow plenty of time for the person to respond (this could be 30 seconds or more)
- check that the person has understood – maybe ask them to explain it back to you
- be aware of the impact of the environment on communication – background noise or distractions can distort the message and make things harder to understand.

It is also the case that an individual's expressive and receptive communication can be affected by their experiences, including their mental health. You may find that when an individual is well, they can easily follow what is happening on the television or instructions but when they are unwell this will be more challenging. You may have to make further adaptations to your communication to accommodate these fluctuations. It is estimated that about 40% of people with intellectual disabilities will also have hearing loss and this will affect receptive communication.

Daily living skills

Daily living skills are paramount to enabling independence and autonomy. Many people with intellectual disabilities who are known to specialist health and social care services will have their daily living skills assessed, usually by an occupational therapist to inform support and care interventions and to assist with social care assessments for community care packages. Basic daily living skills include:

- Feeding.
- Toileting.

- Grooming.
- Continence.
- Washing and dressing.
- Walking (slips, trips and falls).
- Transfer skills i.e. from walking aid or wheelchair to bed, bath etc.

Typically, if someone with intellectual disabilities requires support in one or all of these areas then they will receive a substantial care package with dedicated staff to help them. There are also 'instrumental daily living skills' such as:

- Managing finances.
- Handling transportation.
- Shopping.
- Preparing meals.
- Using the telephone or other communication devices.
- Managing medication.
- Housework and basic home maintenance.

Many people with mild intellectual disabilities who can undertake basic living skills will live independently or in supported accommodation with targeted support for instrumental daily living skills. Care and support plans and health and social care assessments completed with the person with intellectual disabilities and any family or carers can be used to guide how to support an individual.

As with communication, it is likely that if a person is experiencing poor mental health then their skills in these areas may deteriorate. It may be necessary to temporarily increase care and support during these times in order to maximise independence and prevent loss of any acquired skills.

Challenging behaviour

Behaviours that challenge, such as aggression, self-injury, rocking or smearing, can have an effect on an individual's life and may place them at risk of social isolation and physical interventions such as restraint, and may increase the likelihood of them being prescribed powerful neuroleptic medications. That said, all behaviours have a legitimate function to the person and they are often the only means by which an individual can make a need known, avoid a situation or get access to something that they couldn't ordinarily get. This may be due to poor communication, understanding, or being unable to be assertive.

Case study: Joe

Joe has intellectual disabilities and autism and he recently started a new activity programme, which he was happy about. However, Joe soon started having problems and would become agitated waiting to go to sessions. Joe's support team decided to look at what might be responsible for this change in behaviour. Before episodes where he became upset, Joe would often ask the time. His difficulties telling the time and waiting for activities appeared to be causing the problem. Staff recognised that the clock was distracting as he couldn't tell when the activity would start, which led him to ask questions and become more agitated. The issue seemed to be the minute hand, which Joe would become fixated with, waiting for the activity to start and not understanding the length of time left to wait. To try and help, the minute hand was removed which meant Joe did not have to worry about the length of time to wait. When the hour hand changed he knew that the next timetabled activity would start.

Sensory impairment

Sensory impairments refer to any difficulties that people experience with their senses, for example hearing or seeing. It is estimated that up to 40% of people with intellectual disabilities have additional hearing loss and that often this is not diagnosed. This can make communication and daily living much more difficult and can affect an individual's behaviour. Annual sight and hearing tests can help to monitor an individual's functioning and enable early intervention if any problems are discovered.

Some people with intellectual disabilities may be hyper- or hyposensitive to sensory stimulation and this can affect daily life. Be mindful of the effects of lighting, touch, sound, smells and tastes on an individual and how they may impact upon them. It may be that simple gestures such as dimming lights or shutting out noise will have an impact on an individual's anxiety levels or behaviour.

What is mental illness?

Introduction

This section explores some of the more common mental disorders, how they are experienced and what can be done to alleviate symptoms. It looks at mood and personality disorders, psychotic disorders and dementia.

Mental illness will significantly affect how a person thinks, behaves and interacts with others, and much like physical illness it can be diagnosed only when certain key symptoms are present, depending on the condition. For some with severe forms of mental illness, a spell in hospital may be required either as a voluntary patient or detained under the Mental Health Act if the person is unwilling to stay and they are considered to pose a danger to either themselves or others.

Mental illnesses are often grouped together into mood disorders, psychotic illness and personality disorder. Examples of these are below.

Mood disorders

Mood disorders such as depression and anxiety are the most common mental illnesses. Everyone will get feelings of depression and anxiety from time to time, which is natural. This will have a minor or major impact on their daily life in terms of their energy levels, motivation and feeling low or unable to cope. Some people will go on to develop mental illness and in the case of depression this is often classified due to its severity as mild, moderate or severe.

Although symptoms can vary widely between individuals, low mood is common to everyone suffering depression. Other symptoms experienced can include:

- Lack of energy.
- Lack of motivation.
- Feeling hopeless.
- Feelings of unworthiness.
- Difficulties making decisions.
- Poor memory.
- Poor concentration.
- Low self-esteem.

In more severe cases of depression, the person may also misinterpret what is happening around them leading to false beliefs, known as delusions. For example the person may believe they are poor and destitute when they are not or that parts of their body are not working. People with severe intellectual disabilities may experience some different symptoms of depression such as persistent crying, hair pulling and skin picking and vomiting.

Treatment often consists of talking therapies and/or medication depending on the severity of the illness. In severe cases, treatments such as electroconvulsive therapy (ECT) may also be used (see p.41). This is a treatment given under a short acting anaesthetic that involves sending a small electric current through the brain. This triggers an epileptic seizure to relieve the symptoms associated with severe depression. Usually these treatments will need to be adapted to take account of cognitive and communication impairments inherent in intellectual disabilities.

Case study: depression

Mr A is 25 years old and lives in a residential home. His staff team describe him as being active and outgoing and always willing to take part in activities around the house and in the community. Mr A has some verbal communication and makes his needs known using some words, gestures and vocalisations.

Staff began to have concerns about Mr A's mental health and they took him to see his GP. They explained that Mr A had stopped initiating conversations and would only reply to them using one or two words; they said that he appeared sad and troubled. Over the last six months, Mr A had started to stay in his bedroom and only come down for meals, however he recently stopped even doing that.

The staff are worried about Mr A because he is losing weight and staying in his bedroom all the time. Mr A's GP is concerned about his weight loss and recommends a blood test which the staff manage to support him to have and which comes back normal. The GP asks the staff questions about Mr A's social circumstances; he finds out that before these changes Mr A's key worker left the home for a new job and that shortly after this the staff team started to notice small changes in Mr A's usual routines and behaviour, and that this gradually escalated over the weeks culminating in Mr A's initial appointment. The GP suspects that Mr A might be experiencing a grief reaction to the loss of his key worker, this would usually be considered a normal human emotion, but because Mr A's behaviours are becoming more severe, he is losing weight, refusing meals and not sleeping, he diagnoses a reactive depression and recommends that Mr A access adapted grief counselling and prescribes anti-depressant medication.

Everyone experiences anxiety and it is considered a normal human response to certain situations. However sometimes anxiety occurs where there is no threat and interferes with the person's mental wellbeing. It can be intense and affect the person's ability to perform everyday tasks. It is different from normal anxiety and can induce fear and panic in the person that is recurring and can last over weeks in severe cases. Anxiety is also common for people suffering with depression. When well, anxiety can warn us of potential danger and it keeps us alert to what is around us. Common symptoms of anxiety include physical symptoms such as feeling nauseous, breathlessness, sweating, pains, palpitations and tremors. Other symptoms can include:

- irritability
- excessive worrying
- difficulties concentrating
- fear
- panic
- catastrophic thinking.

Treatment often consists of talking therapies such as cognitive behavioural therapy (CBT) and/or medication depending on the severity of the illness. These treatments will usually need to be adapted to take account of cognitive and communication impairments inherent in intellectual disabilities.

Psychotic disorders

Some people with depression may also experience periods of elation or hypomania. This is commonly known as bipolar disorder. This is characterised by mood swings, which can range from severe lows (depression) to severe highs (mania). When someone is manic or hypomanic they may present with:

- feelings of grandiosity
- raised self-esteem and over confidence
- talking rapidly (pressure of speech)
- racing thoughts (pressure of thought)
- delusions
- hallucinations
- acting irrationally e.g. sexual disinhibition, over spending.

Bipolar disorder is a psychotic disorder. A general rule for this group of illnesses is that the person will lose touch with reality. Around 1% of people are thought to suffer from psychotic disorders such as schizophrenia (NIMH, 2016). For people with intellectual disability this is thought to be as high as 3%. These disorders are often referred to as 'severe mental illnesses'.

Schizophrenia and psychosis affects and distorts the person's sense of reality across their senses and can affect all the senses – sight, smell, taste, touch and sound – in the form of hallucinations and delusions. The most common hallucinations are auditory, often described as hearing voices. At their worse, these can be very distressing and encourage the person to do things against their will. They can also be critical of the person and their life. In some cases voices are incorporated as part of a person's life. The person with psychosis can also suffer from delusions and can believe someone is harming them (more common in paranoid schizophrenia) or that they have some divine powers. These symptoms are usually present in the acute phase. In chronic schizophrenia the presentation can be quite different with the person suffering residual or fleeting symptoms and the illness is characterised by negative thoughts, lack of motivation and interest in their surroundings. Other symptoms include:

- difficulties in determining what is real or not
- muddled thinking and speech
- difficulty in relating to others
- poor motivation

- self-neglect
- poor self-care.

People with intellectual disabilities can experience psychotic illness and some may experience different signs and symptoms to the wider population. For example, the more severe the intellectual disability then the more likely that signs of a psychotic disorder may present 'behaviourally', for example with aggression and/or self-injurious and self-harming behaviours. For people with mild intellectual disabilities it may be that the content of delusions and hallucinations is less elaborate than the wider population and could be mistaken for infantile like fantasies. This is because people with intellectual disabilities will often not have had access to the same life opportunities and experiences of the wider population.

Case study: schizophrenia

Olayemi is a 19-year-old man with intellectual disabilities. Over the past few weeks his family and friends have noticed increasingly bizarre behaviour at college, such as whispering to himself and becoming easily agitated. Over the last week he has refused to attend sessions in the computer labs as he thinks that the people who work there are imposters who don't want him there.

The college welfare department have called Olayemi's parents with their concerns and have recommended he see his GP. In the last few days he has gone to the door of the library and warned other students not to go in as something might happen to them. His parents have tried to get him to go with them to a psychiatrist for an evaluation, but he refuses. Concerned for him and his behaviour, the college have suspended Olayemi. He eventually sees his GP who sends him to see a psychiatrist who believes Olayemi has an early stage of schizophrenia. After starting on medication Olayemi improves. The psychiatrist works with college welfare and makes a plan with Olayemi for what to do if the strange thoughts start to reoccur or become too distressing. This is helpful for Olayemi who has difficulty recognising or talking about 'things' that happen to him.

Personality disorders

As well as mental illness, another serious mental health problem is personality disorder. It is estimated that around 10% to 13% of the general population have a personality disorder. For people with intellectual disability this has always been a contentious diagnosis. Recent estimates suggest people with intellectual disabilities suffer at higher rates of certain kinds of personality disorder. Personality disorders are characterised by maladaptive and anti-social patterns of behaviour, have had to have occurred from childhood and are a natural response for the person to situations of adversity etc. People are often misdiagnosed due to how they behave in a given adverse situation. However, this is not normally how they cope with other life situations or how they interact with and respond to others. Personality disorder is not only a difficult concept to understand but also one that is often used negatively to describe people whose actions challenge our patience.

Common to different types of personality disorders are inflexible and unhealthy patterns of behaviour that affect a person's actions, feelings and behaviours that have developed form childhood; and not just poor behaviour in a bad situation. People with personality disorders may blame others for mistakes or what is going on around them, often alienating others.

Personality disorders tend to become apparent in the teenage years or early adulthood. For people with intellectual disabilities a diagnosis may not be possible until adulthood due to late development and reaching maturity which are conditions that have to be considered. There are a number of different types of personality disorder, so symptoms will vary depending on the type.

The different types of personality disorder include:

- Paranoid.
- Schizoid.
- Dissocial.
- Emotionally unstable (impulsive and borderline types).
- Histrionic.
- Anankastic.
- Dependent.

Below is a brief description of some of the more common personality disorders.

Paranoid personality disorder

This is characterised by being suspicious of others. There may be feelings that they are out to do you harm or just want to use you and take advantage. This makes it difficult to develop relationships given difficulties with trust. They will also see danger in certain situations not apparent to others, such as suspecting that a partner is being unfaithful, with no evidence or reading threats and danger into everyday situations which others don't see.

Dissocial personality disorder

People with dissocial PD are likely to act impulsively with no thought of the consequences to themselves or others. They are also likely to get into trouble with the law and more likely to behave dangerously and/or illegally than others. Often they will put their needs before those of others and often have no sense of guilt for their actions.

Borderline personality disorder (BPD)

People in this group can be described as changeable – they may appear temperamental, go through mood changes and suffer from brief and transient psychotic symptoms such as hallucinations. Like other personality disorders, people can be impulsive which affects relationships with those around them who may feel they are being tested due to the erratic nature of the person's behaviour. This might include self-harm or testing others.

Traditionally there has been a reluctance to give this diagnosis to people with intellectual disabilities as it is seen as stigmatising and unhelpful and a barrier to receiving services. However, increased awareness has now meant that there are specialist services being developed for those with personality disorder.

Case study: personality disorder

Rani is a 35-year-old woman who was admitted to A&E after cutting her wrists and taking an overdose of painkillers. For most of her adult life she has felt alone and not had any proper or meaningful relationships. Although she has liked people, often her behaviour has caused these friendships to break up. Rani believes those around her do not understand her and she has been critical of and angry and sullen towards others trying to help her. In the last week, following a review meeting and before going to hospital, she started shouting at people and engaging in impulsive behaviours like running away from home. Staff at the house had become concerned about her as she had also become increasingly emotional and subject to rapid mood changes which were difficult to predict. At A&E Rani was seen by a psychiatrist who prescribed her an antidepressant for her low mood and referred her to a psychologist to work on some of her issues. Since going to see the psychologist Rani still feels overwhelmed at times and gets angry. However, this is not as often nor as bad as before. Rani puts this down to new strategies and coping skills she has learned to help her be in control and manage her symptoms.

Dementia

Dementia describes a set of symptoms involving different neurological disorders. It is a progressive disorder which means that the severity of the symptoms increases with time. People with dementia often experience difficulties with their:

- memory
- language and communication
- behaviour and mood changes.

For example, an individual may experience problems with their short term memory and find it difficult to retain new information; they may become confused and disorientated in familiar environments and experience poor concentration, restlessness or pacing; they may also have difficulties finding words or repeat themselves, and because of these difficulties some people might start to avoid social situations or lose interest in people and things.

People with intellectual disabilities are at an increased risk of developing dementia and they are more likely to get it at a younger age with a faster progression than others. People with Down's syndrome are more likely to get dementia than people with other types of intellectual disabilities. It is important that people with Down's syndrome are regularly assessed for signs of dementia from an earlier age than the wider population (in their 30s or 40s) and that an accurate functional skills assessment is undertaken so that any changes which could be due to dementia can be assessed at a later stage.

There is no cure for dementia and treatment should focus on ensuring good support and the right environment to make the person feel more comfortable. Regular health checks should be undertaken and a multiprofessional team of health and social care professionals can support individuals and their families or carers to address specific difficulties. Medication can sometimes be prescribed by a doctor that can slow down the progression of dementia.

Case study: dementia

Annie is 64 years old and lives in supported housing. She works at a local charity shop for two afternoons a week. Over the past six months, staff at the charity shop and Annie's support workers have noticed that she doesn't seem to enjoy working anymore and that she will try to avoid going to work.

A community nurse meets Annie and talks to her about this. Annie becomes upset and says that she doesn't want to go to work anymore as she is 'embarrassed'. When asked more about this she explains that she often forgets how to use the till and has made mistakes with money, and that sometimes she cannot find the toilet even though that was never a problem before. Annie tells the nurse that she is worried about herself and that she does not understand why she can't do the things that she used to.

Annie's support workers have noticed that she has had a number of trips and falls over the past eight weeks and Annie's colleagues noted that she has started to struggle to join in with conversations and gets muddled up, whereas previously she would happily sit and chat to everyone.

Annie agrees to let the nurse make a referral to her local intellectual disability dementia pathway for an assessment.

Mental health assessment for people with intellectual disabilitie

Introduction

The assessment of mental health is often standardised and involves a clinical interview aimed at detecting symptoms. For people with intellectual disabilities this process can often miss mental health issues or illness. This occurs for a number of reasons; perhaps because the person is a poor reporter of what is happening to them, or the symptoms they present with are missed as they are not typical or generally associated with a specific mental health need. Mental health problems may also be missed when mental illness is wrongly associated as part of their intellectual disability.

Multi-professional care

The care and treatment of mental illness in an individual with an intellectual disability is carried out by multi-professional teams and will often involve different agencies, for example health and social care, and different healthcare professionals will lead on different aspects of the assessment, care and treatment. Typically, a psychiatrist will assess an individual's mental state, make a diagnosis, prescribe medication and provide follow up appointments and medication reviews. They will likely liaise with GPs and other doctors who may be involved in the person's care. Nurses may monitor behaviours and mental state as well as provide support with medication management and co-ordinate care around the person. Social workers help and protect vulnerable people and support them to live independently, while psychologists and behaviour support may assess and provide talking and behavioural therapies; occupational therapists may assess daily living skills and functioning and make recommendations for support and skill development; and speech and language therapists (SLTs) can provide communication assessments and enhanced communication methods to facilitate assessment and treatment. All professionals will work together and should endeavour to involve family and carers.

Ways to support someone to access care

When supporting an individual to access mental health services it is important to provide emotional, psychological and practical support. Speak with those providing mental health care and treatment about what is happening and how best to support the individual. You may have to support them to prepare for appointments by ensuring that they have all the information required, for example a list of current medications and support plans, and that they understand who they are seeing and why.

It is important to provide consistent care and support and ensure that all carers are familiar with treatment plans and that everyone carries out any behaviour support plans consistently and as recommended.

Healthcare professionals may ask you to complete monitoring sheets about behaviours or specific signs and symptoms that an individual may be experiencing. Accurate and consistent completion of these charts will assist the assessment process and any subsequent diagnosis and intervention(s).

People with intellectual disabilities will often have many different carers and professionals involved in their daily lives. It is important that information is shared with those involved (with the individual's consent) for continuity of care.

In order for an individual with intellectual disabilities to receive the same standard of service as the wider population it may be necessary to make adjustments to the way that that service is delivered. For example, in much the same way that a ramp may help a wheelchair user access a building, some psychosocial adjustments may be required to enable people with intellectual disabilities to access mental health services. This might mean requesting longer appointment times to enable better communication, or allowing carers to stay in hospital with someone, or providing written information in an alternative format such a pictures.

The NICE guidance *Mental Health Problems in People with Learning Disabilities: Prevention, assessment and management* was published in 2016. This brings together experts to decide on what is best practice after taking into consideration what is currently known. The guidance says that when considering someone's mental health the following should be considered:

- differences in the presentation of mental health problems, for example changes in behaviour
- communication needs
- decision-making capacity – knowing what the person prefers in terms of how they are treated
- the degree of learning disabilities – for many this may impact on how they express their situation, or lead to difficulty for clinicians not used to working with this group
- the treatment setting (for example, primary or secondary care services, mental health or learning disabilities services, in the community or the person's home)
- interventions specifically for people with learning disabilities – these could be assessment tools such as the PAS-ADD, Glasgow Depression Scale or Glasgow Anxiety Scale, or adapting materials to deliver psychological therapies to make them accessible.

The guidelines also tell us what is required to organise effective care and who should be involved.

'*A designated leadership team of healthcare professionals, educational staff, social care practitioners and health and local authority commissioners should develop and implement service delivery systems in partnership with people with learning disabilities and mental health problems and (as appropriate) their family members, carers, self-advocates or care workers.*'

(NICE, 2019, p8)

The multi-agency designated leadership team should ensure that care is:

- person-centred and integrated within a care programme
- negotiable, workable and understandable for people with learning disabilities and mental health problems, their family members, carers or care workers, and staff
- accessible and acceptable to people using the services
- responsive to the needs and abilities of people with learning disabilities, and that
- reasonable adjustments (in line with the Equality Act, 2010) are made if needed
- regularly audited to assess effectiveness, accessibility and acceptability.

(NICE, 2019, p9)

The designated leadership team should ensure that care pathways:

- cover all health, social care, support and education services, and define the roles and responsibilities of each service
- have designated staff who are responsible for coordinating:
  - how people are involved with a care pathway
  - transition between services within and across different care pathways
- maintain consistency of care
- have protocols for sharing information with the person with learning disabilities and a mental health problem and their family members, carers or care workers (as appropriate) with other staff (including GPs) involved in the person's care.

(NICE, 2019, p9)

Assessment

For those with mild intellectual disability assessment will be similar or the same to that experienced by the general population. Although adjustment may be required for people to fully participate. Those with severe intellectual disability may have limited communication skills, so for them diagnosis may be more relaintreliant on changes in behaviour and on the observations of others. For example, are there any changes in eating or sleeping? Or is the person responding differently for example increased agitation to situations they would not normally be bothered by? For those who communicate differently or who have difficulty expressing themselves is there another explanation for the current situation e.g. underlying physical illness?

Assessment information

To get a detailed description of someone's mental health problems/needs or mental state it is important to record information related to various parts of the person's life as well as the signs and symptoms, they currently have such as their feelings, thoughts and actions. For example changes we experience from the list below may all affect our mental wellbeing.

- Physical health and wellbeing
- Housing and financial circumstances
- Employment and training needs
- Family/social relationships

For people with intellectual disability there may be other factors that increase the likelihood of mental illness such as genetic conditions or family history of mental health problems. In some cases our gender or ethnicity may increase likelihood of certain condition, for example men with intellectual disability are more likely to get schizophrenia that men without.

Assessment support

It is important that a thorough assessment is completed if you have concerns about a person with intellectual disabilities' mental health. This is because psychiatrists often rely on individual accounts and reporting of symptoms which some people with intellectual disabilities will find more difficult to do. Support is vital to ensure that communication is appropriate to the individual and that they have been given sufficient time to understand and reply to questions. Additionally, you may be required to complete observations of particular behaviours over a period of time to notice any changes and to understand the function of a particular behaviour. Furthermore, a thorough physical health check should also be completed to rule out any physical causes for the changes.

There are a number of things that can be done when supporting someone through the assessment process. These include adaptations to the environment, making the appointment and providing access to information to assist understanding and what is required from carers. Some examples are given in **Table 3.1**.

Table 3.1: Assessment grid

Adaptation	Rationale
Longer appointment times.	To aid improved communication and comprehension.
Appointment times at the beginning or end of the day.	To avoid long waiting times or busy waiting rooms, which can increase anxiety.
Accessible information.	To aid comprehension.
Preparedness – person with intellectual disabilities and staff supporting them. Understand what the appointment is for, bring all relevant information and any communication aids or accessible information that could assist the consultation.	To improve the quality of consultation and enable a comprehensive exchange of information to inform diagnosis, care and treatment.
Talking directly to the individual with intellectual disabilities and only later clarifying with carers or family.	To value and involve the person with intellectual disabilities and provide person centred care.
Adaptation	Rationale

Adaptation	Rationale
Anchoring events i.e. take your medicine after the late night news or 'remember when we did X…' rather than saying '4 weeks ago…'	To enable improved communication.
Environment – free from background noise, flicking lights, and medical equipment that is not required.	To reduce anxiety and improve receptive communication.
Check that the person has understood what you have said by asking them to explain it back to you.	To check comprehension and avoid acquiescence.
If using complex or technical words, check that you both have the same understanding of what is meant by that word.	To avoid misdiagnosis or diagnostic overshadowing and facilitate communication.
Consider using pictures or symbols to augment verbal communication.	To aid comprehension.
Make the environment as friendly and predictable as possible or complete the assessment at a venue that the person feels most comfortable in.	To reduce anxiety and increase rapport.
Ask the same questions in different ways at different times during the appointment.	To check comprehension and avoid acquiescence.
Ensure that you fully understand what the concerns or difficulties are and that you fully understand what is normal for the person with intellectual disabilities. Act on any changes that are reported and consider possible physical or mental health diagnoses.	To avoid diagnostic overshadowing and ensure timely access to appropriate healthcare.
Conduct a thorough assessment of mental and physical health, which could include: • physical examination and appropriate investigations • medication history (neuroleptics, anti-hypertensives, steroids etc.) • adverse effects of drugs (including anti-depressants)	Differential diagnosis and diagnostic overshadowing. Sometimes people with intellectual disabilities can experience different or 'atypical' signs and symptoms of illnesses or they seek help at a late stage of an illness which makes it appear different to how it might usually present.

- assessment to exclude other differential diagnoses.

Risk assessment (for both self-harm, self-neglect, harm to others and adult safeguarding) is important.

This can mean that serious illness is not diagnosed or incorrectly diagnosed leading to delays in treatment.

Following assessment there will usually be a number of treatment options depending on the diagnosis.

Mental health interventions and treatment for people with intellectual disabilities

Introduction

Treatment options should not only depend on the diagnosis, but also take into account the individual's preferences. These preferences are often by what people tolerate well e.g. talking therapies where possible, if drugs are necessary then drugs with fewer side effects. This chapter looks at common treatment approaches, beginning with psychological treatments then going onto physical treatments such a medication.

Common treatment approaches

Psychological interventions/talking therapies

Psychological therapies are a treatment where an individual speaks to a trained therapist about their problems who assists the person to overcome them. Depending on the interventions used, these treatments may offer time to reflect, let the person be listened to, help the person understand their situations or help them understand that their thoughts may affect their behaviour. It is only in recent times that interest in and acceptance of the use of psychological therapies in people intellectual disabilities has garnered favour. The UK government's mainstream agenda has meant that more people with intellectual disabilities are accessing generic mental health services and therefore the range of therapies that are on offer, albeit with adaptions to enable access. They may be delivered individually, in a group, systemically– with carers/family/staff, in person or online.

Positive behaviour support (PBS)

Positive behaviour support (PBS) is a process used to understand the reasons for challenging behaviours, identify triggers and put in place a programme of support to reduce those behaviours and their impact. PBS believes that all behaviours have a function and are maintained by responses to them. PBS seeks to understand those behaviours and find alternative, adaptive means of achieving the function. This might be through improved communication, improved problem solving and coping skills, increasing social and meaningful activities and consequently reducing risk of harm and social isolation. PBS plans should be proactive and aim to stop the need for the behaviour occurring but they also offer reactive plans that can minimise the use of restrictive physical interventions.

Cognitive behavioural therapy (CBT)

Cognitive behavioural therapy (CBT) is a popular psychological therapy that supports people to explore the links between their thoughts, feelings and behaviours, and how these influence each other. It can be used to treat a number of mental and physical health and behavioural difficulties. CBT works by helping us to think about situations and how we respond to them and it encourages us to recognise that the way we think and feel about situations influences our behaviour.

For example, Joe has depression and because of this he can view things in a negative way. He walks down a busy high street when he sees his friend Mike walking up on the other side of the road. Joe waves and calls out to Mike who does not respond. Joe feels sad (feeling) and thinks that Mike did this deliberately because he is angry with him for something (thoughts). He decides that it's best if he avoids Mike for the time being (behaviour) as he must have done something wrong. Joe meets with his therapist and talks about the incident. His therapist asks him to think about alternative explanations for why Mike did not wave back to him. Joe is able to recognise that the high street was very busy with cars and buses and that his friend may not have seen or heard him (thoughts) and that his friend has always been very supportive and they've haven't argued, so how could he be angry with him (feelings)? Joe decides to telephone Mike for a chat and tell him about the high street (behaviour).

CBT can be adapted to meet the needs of people with intellectual disabilities and can be delivered by CBT psychologists, therapists or clinical. Adaptations for people with intellectual disabilities might include longer or shorter sessions, more sessions closer together, support with communication, support with homework activities such as keeping a mood diary or testing out scenarios, easy read information and pictures or symbols. Some people with mild intellectual disabilities will be able to access CBT from mainstream services available at a GP surgery or their local IAPT team (Improving Access to Psychological Therapies). Those with more severe intellectual disabilities or specific communication needs may need to access this therapy from specialist intellectual disability services.

Mindfulness

Mindfulness is a practice being increasingly used as part of psychotherapy in the UK that involves a person being totally absorbed in the present moment and acknowledging their thoughts and feelings without judgement and with acceptance. There are three core components to mindfulness: self-reflection, mind-body relaxation, and self-regulation. These three components can be adapted to meet the needs of people with intellectual disabilities using different techniques such as progressive muscle relaxation, meditation and yoga. Mindfulness in the wider population has been shown to be effective in managing symptoms of anxiety, depression, anger and stress, and initial research about mindfulness and intellectual disabilities has shown similar positive effects. Its simplicity and effectiveness means that it can be easily transferred into care settings for use by people with intellectual disabilities and/or their carers.

Guided self help

Guided self help (GSH) is a treatment aimed at prevention, early detection and helping people cope with mental health problems. It is a recognised treatment for mild depression and anxiety (NICE, 2009). GSH is supported by a facilitator who may be a nurse or health worker and who uses different methods such as self-help books and manuals to help the person manage their own mental health.

One GSH package for people with intellectual disabilities is the Self Assessment and INTervention Package, known as the SAINT. The SAINT can be used either independently or with support and is designed to help the person to monitor their mental health through self-report and by learning to recognise and prompting the reporting of symptoms. It then provides options to manage them by providing a range of coping strategies.

Physical treatment approaches: medication

Whether you are prescribed or offered medication will depend often on the severity of the illness and whether there are any alternatives available, which may be indicated in milder form of illness. When being prescribed medication or supporting someone experiencing mental ill health, there is certain information the doctor will need and which you should be familiar with, such as knowing what medications (including items such as herbal or vitamin supplements) the person is currently taking or has been taking recently, and any sensitivities or allergies they may have. For some people there may be other issues, such as difficulty swallowing tablets or fear of needles for those taking long-acting injections.

When someone is diagnosed with a mental illness, then they may be prescribed medications to treat the illness and/or relieve symptoms. There are different groups of medication that target different types of mental illness, such as anxiety, depression or psychosis. Other medications can also be prescribed to relieve some challenging symptoms such as anger, aggression or poor sleep. If medications are prescribed you should make sure that you have information about:

- the name of the medication and what it is prescribed for
- how long the medication should be taken for and when it will be reviewed
- how you will know if it is working
- any side effects or potential drug interactions and what to do about them
- how to take the medication.

A medication review should be undertaken at least once a year for those who are on long-term prescriptions.

There are four main types of medication used in the treatment of mental illness:

- Antidepressants, most commonly used in the treatment of depression but may also relive anxiety or be useful in eating disorders in some cases.
- Anti-psychotics, most commonly used in psychotic illnesses such as schizophrenia, mania or in severe agitation.
- Mood stabilisers, mostly used in bi-polar disorders but some drugs in this group will also be used to treat epilepsy.
- The final group are anxiolytics, which have commonly been over prescribed and can be addictive. They are usually used short term for severe anxiety or insomnia.

Most medications are given in tablet form although for some people with psychosis, long-acting injections might be used. The main benefits of these are that they assist treatment adherence i.e. knowing the person is getting the correct dose and in some cases stopping the need to take medications at set times throughout the day. **Table 3.2** provides some examples of medication commonly used to treat mental illness.

Table 3.2: Examples of commonly used medication for mental illness

Drug group	Generic name	Manufacturer name	Side effects
Antidepressants	Citalopram Fluvoxamine Paroxetine Fluoxetine Sertraline Clomipramine Amitriptyline Venlafaxine	Celexa Luvox Paxil Prozac Zoloft Anafranil Elavil Effexor	Nausea and vomiting Weight gain Diarrhoea Sleepiness Sexual problems
Anti-psychotics	Clozapine Haloperidol Risperidone Quetiapine Trifluoperazine Olanzapine	Clozaril Haldol Risperdal Seroquel Stelazine Zyprexa	Drowsiness Dizziness Restlessness Weight gain Dry mouth Constipation Nausea Vomiting Blurred vision Low blood pressure Seizures People on antipsychotics will need regular physical checks, including blood tests for white blood cell count. These fight infection and low white cell count is a common side effect. The person should also have their weight, glucose levels and lipid levels monitored regularly by a doctor.

Drug group	Generic name	Manufacturer name	Side effects
Anti-psychotics (continued)			For some of the older brands of anti-psychotics, such as chlorpromazine and haloperidol, side effects may include Parkinson's disease type symptoms including: Tics. Tremors. Rigidity. Muscle spasms. Restlessness.
Mood stabilisers	Lamatrogine Lithium Carbonate Carbamazepine	Lamictal Lithium, Tegretol Carbotrol	Lithium can cause several side effects which can be serious. Because of this, those prescribed lithium will require regular blood test of lithium levels. Over recent years there has been an increase in prescribing drugs traditionally used for epilepsy which are also mood stabilisers. Side effects include: Itching and rash Excessive thirst which can lead to excessive drinking Frequent urination Tremor (shakiness) of the hands Nausea and vomiting Slurred speech Fast, slow, irregular, or pounding heartbeat

Drug group	Generic name	Manufacturer name	Side effects
Mood stabilisers (continued)			Blackouts
			Seizures
			Hallucinations
			Confusion
			Swelling of the eyes, face, lips, tongue, throat, hands, feet, ankles, or lower legs.
Anxiolytics	lorazepam buspirone clonazepam diazepam alprazolam	Ativan BuSpar Klonopin Valium Xanax	Nausea Blurred vision Headache Confusion Tiredness Nightmares

Electroconvulsive therapy (ECT)

Electroconvulsive therapy (ECT) is used when other treatment methods have failed for people with severe depression and is used where there is a risk to life or further serious deterioration of a person's condition. In some cases it is also used to treat mania.

ECT works by sending an electric current through the brain to trigger an epileptic fit. To reduce the fit to a fine tremor, a muscle relaxant is used and the procedure is given under a general anaesthetic. For many, ECT has an almost immediate effect.

ECT may, however, bring its own issues – the person may be more able to act on thoughts of harming themselves due to increased motivation. Support is therefore necessary both during and between sessions. A number of people who have ECT complain about memory loss or, for those who have had this treatment previously, believe that they feel there memory is not as good as it used to be.

Principles of intervention

Whatever the intervention these should be based firmly on the outcome of the assessment and should be aimed at:

- Reducing signs and symptoms.
- Reducing distress to the individual.
- Reducing likelihood of relapse.

- Should aim at increasing social inclusion.
- Should include a range of interventions based on the bio psychosocial model.
- Should be multi-professional.
- should aim at reducing vulnerability factors and increasing protective factors.
- Should be regularly reviewed and evaluated.

Mental health promotion and the views of people with intellectual disabilities

Introduction

Central to providing good mental health care is listening to the experiences of others. Mental health promotion can be more effective and meaningful when it is tailored to specific groups and shared experiences. For example, we know that people with intellectual disabilities often have trouble accessing health services across the board when compared to others. The focus of good mental health promotion should not only be on reducing symptoms, but should start with promoting a lifestyle that promotes mental wellbeing and supporting people to have the confidence to engage with services.

The Tuesday Group: a mental health promotion group for people with intellectual disabilities

People with intellectual disabilities are vulnerable to developing mental health problems due to an interaction of biological, psychological and social factors. This vulnerability has led to a concentration on detecting, assessing and treating mental health problems in this population. The situation is worsened by high levels of unmet need which are often poorly identified. Little attention has been given to what can help protect people with intellectual disabilities from mental health problems, resulting in specific programmes to promote positive mental health being sparse. This section describes the development, implementation, evaluation and evolvement of a mental health promotion group for people with intellectual disabilities (called the Tuesday Group) for people with intellectual disabilities.

Mental health promotion

Mental health promotion involves any action, thoughts, intentions etc. to enhance the mental wellbeing of individuals and their families. Mental health promotion initiatives may also be targeted at organisations or communities in the form of public health campaigns. Good mental health promotion strategies aim to minimise the effects of vulnerability factors, while increasing the individual's protective factors in order to prevent illness and reduce the likelihood of relapse. Strategies can range from those that seek to improve housing and the local environment, to those focused on individuals that may offer access to information, education, individual coping skills and community participation among others. A wide range of stakeholders, from government to local authorities, employers to families, and of course the individual themselves, are involved in the implementation of strategies. The argument for adopting a proactive model to mental health is strong; it improves the individual's quality of life, increases productivity and reduces the need for state intervention.

Due to the increased rates of mental health problems among people with intellectual disabilities, proactive strategies are essential and should not be viewed as secondary to treatment and only incorporated within an individual's life once people are unwell. Mental health promotion can be complex with a number of components, and may include:

- managing change
- modifying the environment
- making contact with other people and developing relationships
- recognising, understanding and communicating thoughts and feelings
- managing negative and positive experiences and feelings (stress and adversity)

- believing in their ability or capacities e.g. experiencing achievements
- developing feelings of self-worth.

The Tuesday Group was set up to help support people with intellectual disabilities to develop, practice and learn these skills. The group was formed following consultation with a local service user organisation on what support people with intellectual disabilities wanted for their mental health. A common theme was a need for support groups and information about mental health problems and how people can stay mentally well. This led to the development of a mental health promotion course.

Development of the group

Aims and objectives

The first task was to establish exactly what the course should achieve, which was based on what the group thought would help them stay mentally well. This included:

- learning ways to relax
- knowing what can make you depressed or anxious
- having information about mental health and services
- speaking up for yourself.

The overall aim of the course was to improve the mental health of the group members and to try and achieve the following outcomes:

- To enable group members to recognise their own emotions and feelings and identify situations that they might find stressful.
- To help group members to cope with stressful events more effectively.
- To raise group member's awareness of non-psychotic illness, especially depression and anxiety.
- To provide group members with information regarding the range of services available in their local area, not only clinical services, but also leisure, advocacy and support services.

The first group comprised a ten-week course of two-hourly sessions and was primarily aimed at reducing or preventing the likelihood of people developing depression (non-psychotic) and anxiety disorders. The sessions were heavily influenced by putting forward known protective factors and included:

1. General introduction, getting to know each other, establishing ground rules.
2. Understanding and recognising your emotions, especially those associated with depression/anxiety, and the situations in which they might occur.
3. Depression and how it can affect you.

4. Personal factors and preventive strategies.
5. Anxiety and how it can affect you.
6. Personal factors and preventive strategies.
7. What happens if someone becomes mentally ill?
8. Developing individual positive mental health plans.
9. Continuation of session eight.
10. Review of the course.

Various techniques were used to enhance learning including roleplay, which was used to practice difficult and anxiety provoking situations. Homework included asking members to find pictures from magazines with people showing different emotions. The members also benefited from discussing a number of case scenarios that might mirror some of their experiences in some small way, for example a young man with intellectual disabilities becoming anxious after starting at a new day service. One method that was particularly useful was using video clips from popular TV series – these included a person being bullied, a bereavement and a couple breaking up. In session seven, a psychiatrist joined the group and roleplayed (with a group facilitator) what happens in a mental health assessment. Published health promotion materials were also used and simple relaxation was also practised. The course equipped members with their own information pack which included the work they had done.

What people with intellectual disabilities say

As we have seen, people with intellectual disabilities have mental health needs just like everyone else, and if their mental health needs are not met they can develop a mental health problem. People with intellectual disabilities need information and support about what is good for their mental health. Below is a selection of top tips for good mental health and what is important to the people in the Tuesday Group.

Having a social life

'There's nothing worse than being bored.'

'People need to get out and about, meet new people, go to new places and do new things. People need to get out of the house every day.'

'Having friends is good for mental health.'

'I always plan my week to make sure I have things to do. I go to clubs, to the pub, discos. I have made lots of friends.'

Having relationships

'Having relationships with friends and family is very important.'

'People need to have people they can trust and rely on.'

'Having someone to share worries with is good for mental health.'

'Having someone special is also important.'

'I met my fiancée some years ago. She is very special to me.'

'I have been married for 11 years. It wasn't easy to get married in the beginning. The staff tried to stop us getting married; they cancelled the wedding without telling me. We got there in the end, we are still happily married.'

Having a job

'Having a job is important.'

'It gives people something to do, it keeps them busy.'

'People get paid and can buy the things they want.'

'People get respect if they have a job.'

'People get to meet other people and make new friends.'

'I train lots of staff about mental health and I give talks at conferences. It's good to have people listen to what we have to say, it makes me feel proud.'

'Having a job gives you confidence and good self-esteem.'

Looking after yourself

'People should look after their body; a healthy body helps keep the mind healthy.'

'Eating a healthy diet and regular exercise are good for mental health.'

'People with learning disabilities need information and support about healthy eating, exercise, alcohol and what to do if they feel unwell.'

'Carers and support workers need to help people make health plans.'

'Good personal hygiene is very important and it's good for physical health and self-esteem.'

'I try to walk as much as I can and I sometimes go swimming.'

'I have a community nurse who helped write a diet plan for me.'

Speaking up for yourself

'People with learning disabilities sometimes get forgotten or are not listened to.'

'People need to speak up for themselves and let people know what they think.'

'Being assertive is good for your mental health.'

'People with learning disabilities should know what their rights are.'

'I'm an MP for Speaking Up in Lewisham. I wrote a speech about what I wanted to change and people voted me in.'

'I stand up for people's rights. I have given speeches before to the councillors at the Town Hall, I think they listened.'

Keep on learning

'People need to keep their minds healthy.'

'Learning new things keeps the mind healthy and keeps a person on their toes.'

'There should be opportunities to go to college or night classes.'

'Learning new skills that help job prospects.'

'I have learned lots of things at college, like crochet and basket weaving.'

'I have been learning to read, this will help me get a job.'

'You never stop learning.'

Feeling safe

'People need to feel safe in their home and out in the community.'

'People shouldn't feel anxious in their own homes.'

'It's important to know what to do if something goes wrong.'

'A police officer came to our group and talked to us about feeling safe. It was really helpful.'

Final thoughts

'People with learning disabilities have the same rights as anyone else.'

'They have mental health needs and if things go wrong they can develop mental health problems.'

'People need the right support to stay well.'

Strategies for supporting people with mental illness

Given these personal insights, the Tuesday Group provide strategies designed to help those supporting people with mental illness which cover the following areas.

What's the best way for me to treat someone else with mental health problems?

- When someone is distressed, unwell or acting strange, what should people do to help them?
- What are the things to avoid doing or saying that may make the situation worse?

How can people help me?

- Involving people in my care and recovery.
- Listening to what I have to say and find out about me.
- Treating me equally, involving me, and remembering that I am a person.
- What if I get into trouble when I am not well?

Seeing health professionals

- Using questionnaires to find out how I am feeling.
- Giving my nurse or doctor information about me.
- What to do if you don't understand or forget what people are talking about?
- Why do they want to see me again?

There are different approaches for mental health promotion, other approaches include:

Mindapples model

The Mindapples model (on looking after your mental and physical wellbeing) is new in terms of delivery to people with intellectual disabilities. A group was designed and delivered to a group of people with intellectual disabilities in South London. The concept of Mindapples started back in 2008 as an online campaign to ask everyone what they do that's good for their minds just as we would for physical health. The group currently running is facilitated by intellectual disability nurses, a Mindapples facilitator and an expert by experience (person with lived experience of intellectual disability and mental illness). It is an informal group where there is opportunity for the members to co-facilitate different sessions. The activities include a mixture of arts and crafts, visiting speakers on related subjects, learning about wellbeing subjects, promoting inclusion and giving feedback/ suggestions on national strategies and guidelines.

Mental health promotion specifically aimed at people with intellectual disabilities is an emerging area with new approaches still being developed. For example one initiative to help the wider community and those without access to mental health groups is peer mentoring, currently being developed by the Foundation for People with Learning Disabilities, where people with intellectual disability are trained with a non-ID buddy to deliver peer mentoring sessions and mental health awareness to their peers within their own home to promote mental wellbeing.

References

NHS Choices (2016) *Five Steps to Mental Wellbeing* [online]. Available at: http://www.nhs.uk/conditions/stress-anxiety-depression/pages/improve-mental-wellbeing.aspx (accessed September 2016).

NIMH (2016) *Schizophrenia* [online]. Available at: http://www.nimh.nih.gov/health/publications/schizophrenia-booklet-12-2015/index.shtml (accessed September 2016).

WHO (2014) *Mental Health: A state of well-being* [online]. Available at: http://www.who.int/features/factfiles/mental_health/en/ (accessed September 2016).

Useful web links

Alzheimer's Society
www.alzheimers.org.uk

Anxiety UK
www.anxietyuk.org.uk

Bipolar UK
www.bipolaruk.org.uk

Borderline Personality Disorder Resource
http://bpdresourcecenter.org/

CALM – Campaign Against Living Miserably, for men aged 15-35.
www.thecalmzone.net

Depression Alliance
www.depressionalliance.org

Eating disorders
www.b-eat.co.uk

Mental Health Care
www.mentalhealthcare.org.uk

Mental Health Foundation
www.mentalhealth.org.uk

Mind
www.mind.org.uk

OCD Action
www.ocdaction.org.uk

OCD UK
www.ocduk.org

No Panic
www.nopanic.org.uk

PAPYRUS Young suicide prevention society.
www.papyrus-uk.org

Rethink Mental Illness
www.rethink.org

Royal College of Psychiatrists – Links to resources for people with intellectual disabilities and mental health problems and their families and carers
http://www.rcpsych.ac.uk/healthadvice/problemsdisorders/learningdisabilities.aspx

Samaritans
www.samaritans.org.uk

Sane
sanemail@org.uk

Time to change – tackling stigma and mental health
http://www.time-to-change.org.uk/mental-health-stigma

Suicide prevention
http://www.prevent-suicide.org.uk
http://grassrootstrainingcic.blogspot.co.uk

Young Minds
www.youngminds.org.uk

Other useful links

Bereavement
www.crusebereavementcare.org.uk

Family Lives
www.familylives.org.uk

Mencap working with people with an intellectual disability, their families and carers.
www.mencap.org.uk

NSPCC
www.nspcc.org.uk

Refuge
www.refuge.org.uk

Rape Crisis
To find your local services phone: 0808 802 9999 (daily, 12-2.30pm, 7-9.30pm)
www.rapecrisis.org.uk

Relationships
www.relate.org.uk

Victim Support
www.victimsupport.org

Addictions

Alcoholics Anonymous
www.alcoholics-anonymous.org.uk

Gamblers Anonymous
www.gamblersanonymous.org.uk

Narcotics Anonymous
www.ukna.org

Other relevant titles by Pavilion

Introduction to Mental Health and Mental Wellbeing for Staff Supporting Adults with Intellectual Disabilities: A training pack
For more information, see https://www.pavpub.com/mental-health/mental-health-staff-supporting-adults-intellectual-disabilities

Mental Health in Intellectual Disabilities (5th Edition): A complete introduction to assessment, intervention, care and support
For more information, see https://www.pavpub.com/learning-disability/ld-mental-health/mental-health-in-intellectual-disabilities-5th-edition

Mental Health Needs of Children and Young People with Intellectual Disabilities (2nd edition)
For more information, see https://www.pavpub.com/mental-health/mental-health-young-people-intellectual-disabilities

I Can Feel Good (2nd edition): DBT-informed skills training for people with intellectual disabilities and problems managing emotions
For more information, see https://www.pavpub.com/i-can-feel-good-2nd-edition

The CaPDID Training Manual:
Caring for people with a personality disorder and an intellectual disability: A training manual using a trauma informed approach
For more information, see https://www.pavpub.com/learning-disability/capdid-training-manual-caring-for-people-with-a-personality-disorder-and-an-intellectual-disability-a-training-manual-using-a-trauma-informed-approach

Supporting the Physical Health Needs of People with Learning Disabilities: A handbook for professionals, support staff and families
For more information, see https://www.pavpub.com/learning-disability/health/supporting-the-physical-health-needs-of-people-with-learning-disabilities

Reflections on the Challenges of Psychiatry in the UK and Beyond
For more information, see https://www.pavpub.com/mental-health/practice/reflections-on-the-challenges-of-psychiatry-in-the-uk-and-beyond

Anxiety and Depression in People with Intellectual Disabilities

For more information, see https://www.pavpub.com/anxiety-and-depression-in-people-with-intellectual-disabilities/

Intellectual Disabilities and Personality Disorder

For more information, see https://www.pavpub.com/intellectual-disabilities-and-personality-disorder/

Guided Self-help for People with Intellectual Disabilities and Anxiety and Depression

For more information, see https://www.pavpub.com/guided-self-help/

Notes

Notes